BEACON to FREEDOM

THE STORY OF A CONDUCTOR ON THE UNDERGROUND RAILROAD

by *Jenna Glatzer*

illustrated by *Ebony Glenn*

CAPSTONE PRESS
a capstone imprint

In the early 1800s, when John Rankin was a boy, slavery was legal in most of the United States. Some white people owned black people and treated them as property.

John's parents thought that was terrible. "How can anyone think that owning a person is acceptable?" his mother questioned. People like her, who fought for the end of slavery, were called abolitionists. They spoke out in public. They published newsletters and books. Many of them helped enslaved people find safety.

John became an abolitionist, too. He grew up to be a church minister who believed slavery was against God's wishes. Being an abolitionist was very dangerous work. Escaped slaves and those who helped them faced punishment—sometimes even death. It took courage. But John had strong beliefs and a strong heart. And he had a bright light that gave people hope and showed them the way to freedom.

The African slave trade to America started in 1619. Black men, women, and children were kidnapped from Africa, shipped to America, and sold like cattle. They had no rights. Families were often split apart. Some slave owners whipped their slaves to keep them in line.

It was against the law in many states to teach enslaved people how to read or write. Slave owners feared that education might cause trouble. With education, slaves might learn how to get laws changed to make slavery illegal everywhere.

John Rankin grew up in Tennessee in the late 1790s. After marrying and becoming a minister in 1814, he moved to the neighboring state of Kentucky. Both states allowed slavery.

In Kentucky John tried to get slave owners to set their slaves free. He urged them to listen to God's word. He wanted them to understand that it was wrong to own other human beings.

But the slave owners said no. They needed slaves to do their fieldwork. Without slaves, they said, their farms would lose money and fail.

John's beliefs weren't welcome in Kentucky. At times he feared for his safety and the safety of his growing family.

But people were more accepting across the river in Ohio. Ohio was a free state, which meant slavery was against the law. John and his wife, Jean, moved their family there in 1822. The small town of Ripley became the Rankins' new home.

After a few years, the Rankin family moved again. They stayed in Ripley but moved into a house on the hill overlooking the Ohio River. The Ohio River ran between Kentucky and Ohio. If escaped slaves could cross the river, they would be on free soil. But crossing was very risky. They had to swim or row a boat in the dark of night so they wouldn't be seen. If caught by slave catchers, they could be beaten.

Not only was it dangerous to try to escape, it was also dangerous to help anyone trying to escape. John and his family did it anyway. They gave people food and clothing. They hid them in their barn. A trap door in the barn floor, covered with hay, opened to a large hiding space.

Even though Ohio was a free state, some people there wanted to own slaves. They had suspicions that the Rankins were helping escaped slaves, but they couldn't prove it. They said horrible things to John and his family. They threw rotten eggs and stones at them.

Every night, John lit a lamp in one of the front windows of his house. He left it burning all night so people seeking freedom would know where to find him. The light shone toward the Ohio River. It was a beacon of hope.

The Rankins were an important part of the Underground Railroad, which wasn't an actual railroad at all. It was a secret network of friendly people and places runaway slaves could go to. The helpers called themselves conductors. "Passengers" traveled from house to house by foot, horse, train, or boat. They traveled until they found the place where they would settle down, either in the northern United States or Canada.

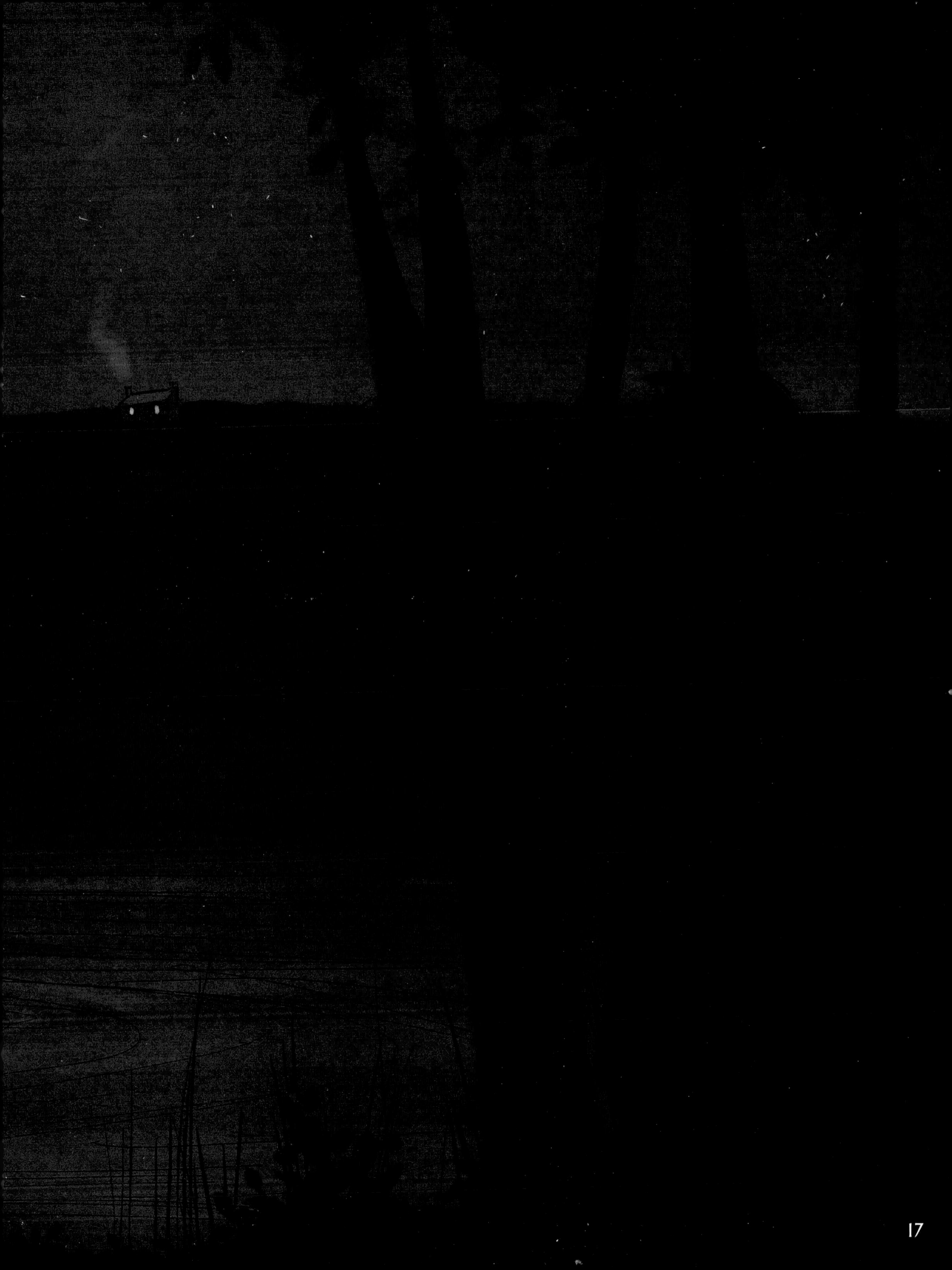

Through the years, John Rankin and his family helped many people. One such person was a woman named Eliza Jane Johnson.

Eliza lived north of Ripley with her husband and five children. One day in 1837, four men on horseback rode up to Eliza's home, whipped her, and stole her away. The main kidnapper, James Fox, thought that Eliza was a slave who had run away from his father's farm in Kentucky four years earlier. He was going to take her back.

The kidnappers raced to the Ohio River. Six men, including John Rankin's oldest son, Lowry, heard Eliza's cries and tried to rescue her. They stopped two of the kidnappers at the river. But the other kidnappers escaped with Eliza in a small boat.

A handful of other men had helped the kidnappers. Lowry later recognized them on his way into town. Filled with anger, he told them, "All women thieves are cowards!" One of the men raised his fist, but Lowry didn't back down. He thought it was especially disgraceful that the kidnappers had waited until Eliza's husband was away to take her.

Once the kidnappers' boat reached the Kentucky side of the river, the men took Eliza to jail. There she spent the night, alone, on the dirt floor of a cell.

The next morning, James Fox's father went to the jail and looked at Eliza. He shook his head. A mistake had been made. She wasn't his runaway slave after all. However, instead of returning Eliza to her family in Ohio, the sheriff kept her in jail. He said that she must be a runaway slave from *somewhere*. She had dark skin. Her color alone made her a slave. She would stay in jail until someone claimed her. And if no one did, he would sell her.

Abolitionists from all over the area, including John Rankin, begged for Eliza's release. John wrote letters to the government. He spoke tirelessly, telling them that Eliza was not someone's property. She was a free woman. She deserved to go back to her family. And finally, after five months in a basement jail cell, Eliza was let go.

The glowing lamp in the window of the Rankins' home helped many enslaved people find courage to escape. They faced great dangers because they knew they would be safe if they got to that house.

In February 1838, an enslaved woman in Kentucky heard terrible news. Her master was thinking of selling his slaves—including her 2-year-old son. She was so terrified of this idea that she set out to cross the Ohio River in the winter cold. She knew there was a man on the other side who could help her and her boy escape.

"Look for the light on the hill," people told her.

The river was not safe to walk on. It was half-frozen, with lots of cracks and holes.

The woman wrapped her child in a blanket and tried anyway.

She fell into the dark, icy water three times, rolling her son onto the ice each time. She was freezing and very weak by the time she made it across the river. But she made it!

Then someone grabbed her arm.

A slave catcher.

The woman thought for sure the man would return her and her son to Kentucky. Slave catchers received good money for runaways. But instead he said, "Any woman who crossed that river carrying her baby has won her freedom." Then he pointed her toward the Rankin house and let her go.

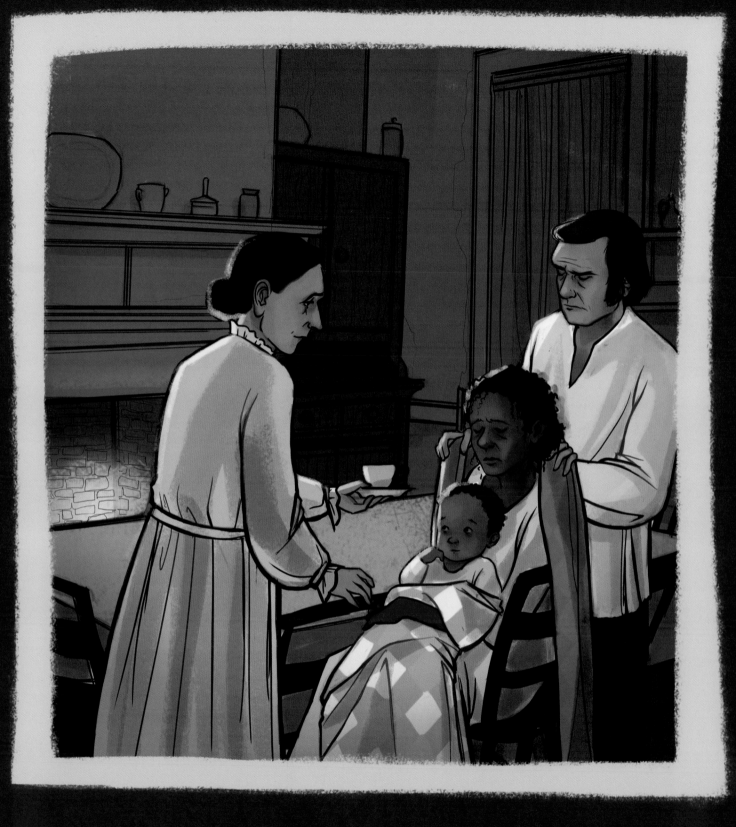

John and his family provided food, warm clothing, and a place to rest. Then they steered the woman and her child on a safe path to Canada. They never found out the woman's name, but they did learn she had left behind a daughter and several grandchildren. She promised that she would go back for them.

Three years later, the woman did return. She came back with a man she'd hired to help her get the rest of her family. John warned that it was too dangerous to go back to Kentucky. If caught, the woman would surely be sold back into slavery. The man would either be jailed or hanged. But she insisted, so John helped her plan the rescue.

Because of kind neighbors and John's sons Samuel and John Jr.,
the woman and her hired man were successful. Everyone, except one
granddaughter, made it safely across the river and eventually to Canada.
Sadly, the granddaughter was a house slave, and there had been no way
to alert her to the rescue.

Not every story on the Underground Railroad had a happy ending. Some runaway slaves did get caught before they made it to the Rankin house or after they left. Sometimes people left their spouses or children behind and planned to return for them later. But that didn't always work. One man rescued his wife and children but was then tricked by a slave catcher pretending to be a friend. The man was captured and shackled.

John sometimes struggled to stay hopeful.
At times he said that he felt

"a sadness so deep that it seemed
as if there was nothing in all
creation could dispel the gloomy
cloud in which I was enveloped."

Posters started appearing that offered a reward for capturing or killing John. Slave owners from Kentucky were furious with him for helping to "steal" their slaves. Slave catchers often snuck around the Rankin land at night, watching for runaways. John feared for his family's safety.

Late one night in 1841, violence broke out. Two pro-slavery men started a fire in the Rankin barn. They meant to burn it down, along with the house and the family members sleeping inside. But John's nephew and sons spotted them in time. They got into a gunfight and eventually scared off the attackers.

John posted a warning in the Ripley newspaper the next day. He spoke to future "midnight assassins."

"I therefore warn all persons to beware lurking about my house and barn at night," he wrote. He said the next time he found intruders on his land, he would shoot them dead.

No other intruders appeared. John and his family continued their work with the Underground Railroad, right through the time of the U.S. Civil War (1861–1865).

For more than 40 years, the lamp at the Rankin house had glowed through the darkness. It had helped nearly 2,000 people find freedom.

AFTERWORD

Abraham Lincoln was elected president of the United States in 1860. He promised to stop the spread of slavery throughout the country. His words were put to the test quickly. After his election, pro-slavery states broke away from the United States to form their own government: the Confederate States of America. The North (Union) and the South (Confederacy) fought the U.S. Civil War from 1861 to 1865. In the end, the North won, and all the states were again united as one country. On December 18, 1865, the 13th Amendment to the U.S. Constitution abolished slavery—246 years after the first Africans were enslaved in America.

With the addition of the 13th Amendment, John Rankin stopped being a conductor. The work he did on the Underground Railroad was no longer needed. He died in 1886 at the age of 93. His house on Liberty Hill in Ripley, Ohio, is now a National Historic Landmark and museum.

GLOSSARY

abolish—to end or do away with

abolitionist—a person who worked to end slavery

assassin—a person who kills a well-known or important person

beacon—a signal to guide or warn people

intruder—a person who enters property without permission

minister—a person who leads a church

network—a system of people or things that cross or connect

organize—to get together to take action

shackle—to bind with chains or handcuffs

spouse—a husband or wife

suspicion—a feeling of doubt or mistrust

U.S. Civil War—(1861–1865) the battle between states in the North and the South that led to the end of slavery in the United States

SOURCE NOTES

Direct quotations come from:

page 20, lines 2–3: Adam Lowry Rankin. *The Autobiography of Adam Lowry Rankin.* Publisher not identified, 1891.

page 31, lines 3–6: John Rankin. *Life of Rev. John Rankin, Written by Himself in His 80th Year c1872.* Ripley, Ohio: Rankin House, 2004, p. 31.

page 34, lines 8–9: Ann Hagedorn. *Beyond the River: The Untold Story of the Heroes of the Underground Railroad.* New York: Simon & Schuster, 2002, p. 221.

INDEX

Thanks to our adviser for her expertise, research, and advice:
Betty Campbell, president of Ripley Heritage, Inc.
and site manager for the Rankin House, Ripley, Ohio.
Additional thanks to Donald Rankin, MD, for giving generously of his time and insights.

Editor: Jill Kalz
Designer: Ashlee Suker
Creative Director: Nathan Gassman
Production Specialist: Tori Abraham
The illustrations in this book were created digitally.

Published by Capstone Press,
1710 Roe Crest Drive, North Mankato, Minnesota 56003
www.mycapstone.com

Library of Congress Cataloging-in-Publication Data
is available on the Library of Congress website.
ISBN 978-1-5157-3496-3 (library binding)
ISBN 978-1-5157-3497-0 (paperback)
ISBN 978-1-5157-3498-7 (eBook PDF)
Summary: Describes the role Reverend John Rankin played in helping people
escape slavery up to and throughout the U.S. Civil War by means of the
Underground Railroad in Ripley, Ohio.

Printed in the United States of America.
010024S17